A Thought Manual for Everyone

(For you too), MAYBE

Nicolas Okin

Copyright © 2023
All Rights Reserved

Dedication

"I dedicate this book to my kids, from whom I learned more than any other human in my life."

Acknowledgments

Writing this book has been a deeply rewarding journey, one that would not have been possible without the support and inspiration of several remarkable individuals. I would like to express my gratitude to the following people:

My Wife: To my life partner, my best friend, and biggest supporter, thank you for your belief in me and your endless encouragement. Your love and patience have been my rock throughout this creative process. Even though you still do not understand my path, your love and support are and always have been the strongest pillars in my life.

My Yoga Teacher: My sincere thanks to my dedicated yoga teacher, who has not only guided me toward physical strength but also imparted invaluable lessons about inner balance.

My Psychologist: I extend my deep appreciation to my psychologist, whose insights into and understanding of my long-lived trauma have enriched my understanding of thoughts and emotions. Your expertise has been a vital source of knowledge for this book.

My Uncle: To my dear uncle, in whom I could confide when times were hard and whose words of wisdom and mentorship helped me more than I could admit.

Each of you has played a significant role in shaping both my personal and creative journey. Your contributions, whether through guidance, emotional support, or expertise, have been instrumental in the creation of this work.

This book stands as a testament to the value of genuine relationships and the infinite power that resides within each and every one of us.

With gratitude,

Nicolas

About the Author

Nicolas Okin is a multifaceted individual with a passion for exploring the intricacies of the human mind. With a deep interest in psychology, philosophy, and spirituality, he has dedicated years to studying the connection between thoughts and personal well-being. Drawing inspiration from both ancient wisdom and contemporary research, Nicolas has crafted a unique perspective on mastering thoughts and fostering mental empowerment.

Nicolas is committed to simplifying complex concepts and providing practical tools to make the work accessible to a wide audience. Having been through anxiety and depression, he is a compassionate advocate for mental health and personal growth. He simply seeks to empower readers to lead more fulfilling lives.

Table of Contents

Important Notice i
Why I Wrote This Book iii
Introduction 1
The Origins of Thought 8
The Truth About Thought 11
Lingering On Thoughts 16
Zoom In And Zoom Out 20
    The Mountain Range 21
    The Garden 23
Managing Emotions 25
    The Opposite Technique (Approach) 25
    The 6 Questions Technique 28
Honest And Sincere Confession 30
There Is No Bad Thought 35
Breaking Free From The Chains Of Compulsive Worrying 40
Breathing Consciously 44
    The 1, 2 Technique 45
    The 1 to 10 Technique 45
    The Narration Technique 47
    The Detailed Breathing Technique 47
    So Ham 49
    Conclusion - Breathing 50
Becoming Conscious Of Thought 52

The Power of Vocabulary	56
Repetition rather than repression	60
Using The Three Simple Words, I…LOVE…YOU	61
Forgive	65
The Ho'oponnoppono "Prayer"	67
Be Thankful	69
Stop Complaining And Let Go Of The Need To Be Right	73
The Five Senses and Thought	76
Smell:	77
Sight:	77
Hearing:	78
Touch:	78
Taste:	78
Conclusion	81
Bibliography	85

"There are eight billion people on this planet, and each and every one of them is perfect just the way they are... then thought gets in the way."

Important Notice

This book is written by an ordinary individual for fellow individuals who are tired of experiencing thoughts that diminish their self-worth.

I wrote this book with a touch of humor and the influence of many different currents of psychology, spirituality, religion, philosophy... All to produce simple exercises, so simple you almost will not believe they work. But believe it, they work.

This book by no means can replace a psychologist or psychiatrist; if you feel you need help or are having suicidal thoughts at any point during your life, seek help, your greatest strength will always come from your willingness to confront your greatest fears and vulnerabilities.

All the exercises in this book might not suit you; select the ones that come to you easily and repeat them over and over until they have the desired effect. It is better to choose one and repeat incessantly rather than get lost in trying out many and never acquiring the desired results. The most difficult part in starting a new habit is exactly that: STARTING IT. However, new habits can be adopted in only a week's time, especially the ones in this book. Keep your eye on the desired results!

Everything you have learned in your life you learned through repetition, why not start learning to have better thoughts.

I encourage you to look at the table of contents and start with whichever chapter sounds most interesting to you; if you read just that particular one and exercise it every day, you are already making huge progress. You can make progress from the inside out (going into your subconscious and facing your demons staying with them and acknowledging that they are part of you), that is hard. And you can make progress from the outside in (consciously changing your thoughts thus changing the way you perceive your surroundings and circumstances), which is what this book will help you do.

Why I Wrote This Book

I wrote this book as a message to my former self. After years of grappling with anxiety and depression, feeling like a victim of circumstances, and receiving support from my wonderful wife, I began to see the world through a different lens.

> *"I went from being a victim of circumstance to a seer of opportunities."*

Having gone through the eye of the needle and come out the other side, I felt something had changed. My perspective shifted, and with it, my life transformed. I came to the profound realization that circumstances do not control my thoughts, words, and actions.

In the following schematic, there are four important dimensions:

1. Thought: defined in the following chapters.
2. Emotions: a feeling in your body, at the same time, influencing thought as well as created and nourished by the same or similar thought.

3. Circumstances: What happens to you.
4. Actions: Everything you do physically.
5. Words: Everything you say.

The predominant perception of the world for most people is something like this (where circumstances are always the cause of the way your life unfolds):

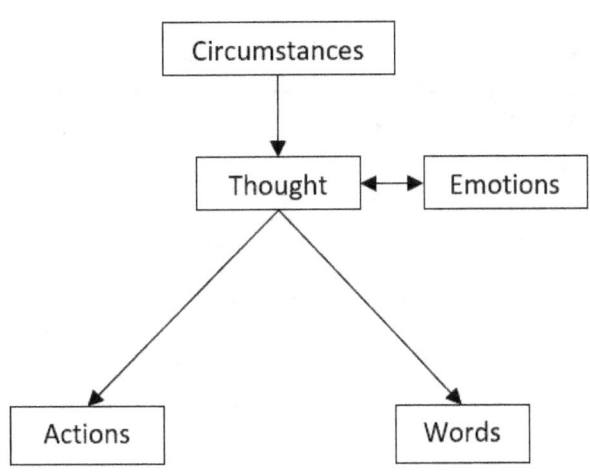

INFLUENCE: ⟶

This process is repeated over and over for every thought, action, and word. From the moment you wake up, your mind is flooded by the enormous amount of information created by your circumstances, forcing us to navigate on autopilot just to get through each day.

But today, I see the world differently:

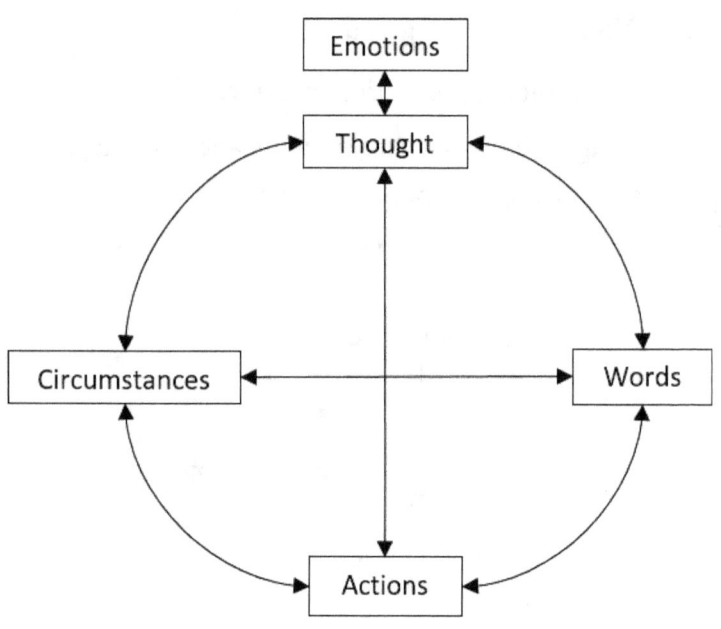

INFLUENCE: ⟵⟶

In this new perspective, circumstances, thoughts, actions, and words all influence each other mutually. With practice, you can learn to influence your surroundings with your thoughts, words, and actions rather than allowing your surroundings to dictate your life.

Using different wording can greatly change the way you perceive the world; what's more, you can choose which words you use! The same goes for actions. Circumstances are harder to change, but if your thoughts, actions, and words stay light and uplifting, there is no circumstance that you cannot get through. Better yet, you will be able, in all circumstances, to see the opportunity.

Most importantly, a single positive thought has the potential to change any circumstance for yourself, and a positive word or action can have an impact as well. It took time and training to implement the mind tricks I share in this book, but they eventually opened the doors to an absolute truth: you are the creator of your own life.

"Everything in your life starts with thought."

Every thought you have, each of the thousands of thoughts that cross your mind every day, are just tiny fragments of who you are, and you are the master of your thoughts. My hope is to equip you with tools that, through repetition, will help you acquire the same vision.

I developed this small manual with several different exercises to help myself get through hard times. I have used all of the exercises in this manual over the last three years and have noticed a great improvement in my relations, interactions, and life in general. All of these exercises might not fit you perfectly; however, repeating one or two every day until they become part of your train of thought has the potential to change your life for the better.

While it is true that circumstances tend to have a greater influence on us during our youth, remember that you possess the power to change the stage on which your life unfolds. Your mind is a fertile ground where any thought can take root, and you have the ability to plant in it whatever thoughts you desire. The first step is to set a new stage.

"You have the power to create any thought by mere repetition of words and actions in your life."

You will finally realize that you are the only one who perceives your thoughts as "bad" or "good," and even that judgment is merely another thought.

Introduction

The person you spend the most time with in your life is yourself. Wouldn't you want to cultivate a relationship with yourself that is loving, respectful, and grateful? Thoughts, as insignificant as they may seem, shape your life and create your reality. They serve as the origin of every action, word, feeling, and interpretation that you go through. Your superpower lies in your ability to control them or, at the very least, keep them under control.

It is crucial to recognize a fundamental truth:

"Thoughts, like everything else in life, are temporary."

And hanging onto any of them, positive or negative, is an exercise in futility (like listening to music while there is a constant sound in the background). In this concise manual, I will present practical tips to help you refine your thoughts. However, remember that without "bad" thoughts, we could never appreciate the "good ones." Your mind is an infinite source of energy that will grow anything you plant within it, whether positive or negative.

You are the only person who will ever know what transpires inside your head. No one else can possibly comprehend your train of thought. So why should you feel guilty, ashamed, or fearful of what occurs within your mind? As long as you haven't acted upon a thought, you cannot be held accountable.

We each have a unique flow of thoughts that make us act the way we do and say the things we say. Thoughts are at the base of every human action, whether it be speaking, doing, inventing, acting, etc… Some of these thoughts are embedded so deep in who we are that getting rid of them is comparable to severing a limb (however, if that limb is the reason you are dying, you would amputate it immediately, no?).

Examples are judgment, comparison, envy, repulsion, homophobia, racism, bigotry, low self-worth, unfairness… We are never born with these thoughts. These will taint your view of the world, preventing you from seeing the beauty of the world as it truly is.

Fantasies, ideas, memories, imagination, planning… all are thoughts. We do not know where they come from or where they go; we equally have no clue. Many come back, and others don't.

Most of your thought process is conditioned by your youth as long as you let it. The way you think and the thoughts that you hold find their roots in your upbringing. Until you become conscious of this, then it is up to you to change the way you think (you have the power to do so).

Each and every one of us has a tendency to dwell on particular thoughts instead of realizing that, like everything else, ALL THOUGHT IS TEMPORARY.

Thoughts are only that; no one can judge you based on your thoughts since no one knows what you are thinking. Why should you judge yourself for certain thoughts that you have? All thoughts are natural to have; what is not natural is feeling guilty, scared, or even angry for having certain thoughts.

Observing them from a distance will help you deal with them on a day-to-day basis. This manual presents methods to choose from in order to be able to see your thoughts and deal with them from a vantage point instead of being submerged by them.

Our ultimate power is our capacity to change our minds at will; however, so few of us are aware of this superpower. Due in great part to childhood conditioning (and conditioning by advertisement, news, TV, and social media...) there are certain thoughts that we think are primordial to our existence: "What will people think?" or "Hard work guarantees success" or "What can I do to be more like him/her?" or constantly comparing your life with others or always finding what is better in the life of others...

The difficulty is being able to see thoughts for what they are: Figments of what Carl Gustav Jung called the collective unconscious. No one knows where they truly come from.

Lingering on a thought gives it unnecessary power over you. Why do we decide to linger on thoughts and get lost in them? Conditioning, addiction, victimization, habit... The truth is you have a choice in what thought you indulge in. The end goal is to not linger on any thought at all. Therefore, enjoy every thought and moment in your life as it presents itself to you. And once it has passed, enjoy the next thought.

From birth, we are told that certain thoughts are prohibited/bad and that a good person does not have these thoughts. How could anybody know what anybody is thinking anyway? What happens when something is forbidden? We automatically create an attachment to it.

"Thoughts can be sparked by exterior stimuli, and unfortunately for us, the exterior stimuli today are mainly lies, bad news, and deceit."

Your thoughts have been influencing your life since you were born, even though most of those thoughts were planted there in your youth by events that are out of your control. For example, our parents, being the people that they are, have a set of pre-established thoughts that even they are not aware of; these were handed down from their parents, and then theirs, and so on.

When you are a child, you are most vulnerable to others' thoughts, words, and actions. This has had an influence over your entire life since you did not have the tools to help you distinguish what was good from what was bad for you. By now, these beliefs have built up huge momentum, and you feel like they are you; THEY ARE NOT.

Eckhart Tolle even goes further and says: "Identification with the mind causes thought to become compulsive. Not being able to stop thinking is a dreadful affliction, but we don't realize this because almost everybody suffers from it, so it is considered normal."(E. Tolle 2004 pp.14).

Identification to a thought is limiting yourself to one potential outcome when there are billions upon billions of outcomes for every situation in life. Simple proof of this fact is that you could get up right now and stand on one foot for five minutes if you wanted to.

"Living in thought is a futility since you are always missing the moment right in front of you."

By the power of your thoughts, every event that happens to you can have a positive impact on your life. Whether you know it or not, you have the power to choose which thoughts come into your mind. That is why this book is a short "manual"; as long as the chosen techniques are not working, you should repeat them incessantly until they do, **and they will**.

You will become the master of your mind and therefore the master of your life.

Hi, I am Lee and I will be accompanying you throughout this manual.

The Origins of Thought

While the exact origin of thoughts remains elusive, various perspectives shed light on this intriguing question: "Where do thoughts come from?"

According to Yohan John, neuroscience PhD, on Forbes.com, from a subjective standpoint, thoughts seem to emerge out of nowhere, popping into our minds or finding expression through spoken words. Objectively, we can attribute thoughts to neural processes, which in turn have intricate connections to various sources.

According to Sadhguru, an eminent spiritual leader, the content of our thoughts is intertwined with the accumulation of our sense perceptions. And in terms of substance, thoughts can be seen as reverberations.

Aldus Huxley, one of the first English writers to explore levels of consciousness, proposed the concept of the mind at large or super-conscious mind, suggesting thoughts emerge from a collective well of consciousness.

Carl Gustav Jung, one of the greatest psychiatrists of all time, talked about the collective unconscious. A vast cradle that holds all past, present, and future thoughts for the entire universe. Our individual minds act as a reducing valve, accessing only portions of this vast reservoir depending on your state of mind at any moment. Once a thought emerges, its source lies within the thought itself. Similarly, water is the source of the river, not the hole in the mountain (if there was the hole but no water, it could not be called a spring, just a hole).

During childhood, the influence of external factors cannot be ignored, people in our surroundings (family members, elders, teachers…) play a significant role in shaping our thoughts through their words, opinions, and perceptions of us. Additionally, advertising, social media, and the media in general inundate us with messages that create false ideals and notions of inadequacy, distorting our self-perception. The mere repetition of these ideas does have an impact on us, but we have the power to select which thoughts will ultimately shape our lives.

While the ultimate source of thoughts remains a mystery, by exploring their origins in your life and understanding the influences at play, we can gain greater clarity and agency over the thoughts that shape our reality.

Come and explore the depth of thought with me

The Truth About Thought

"What sets one free is for another a prison." Jung, 1933, p.48

Thoughts are not you, but they shape your life. This fundamental understanding empowers you to recognize that you have control over your thoughts, even when it may seem otherwise. One thought will never define you as a person. You will always be a complex blend of thoughts, constantly evolving and changing. However, by staying with one thought or a similar group of thoughts, you are preventing this evolution!

Happiness begins with a single happy thought, one that you have the power to create within yourself. Your happiness does not rely on external events or circumstances. John Milton, an intellectual, writer, poet, and fervent defender of human liberty, wrote in his epic poem "Paradise Lost":

"The mind is its own place and in itself can make a heaven of hell or hell of heaven."

The origin of thoughts is mysterious, with some dissipating quickly and others finding their way into your subconscious, paving the way for how you perceive everything in your life.

Remember, all thoughts are temporary. They are products of your imagination, memory, subconscious, and unconscious and are molded by your state of mind. All memories and knowledge stored in your brain are equally recalled as thoughts and are also strongly influenced by your state of mind. The thoughts that you allow to linger in your mind become your reality over time.

It is important to keep an open mind and not let your present perceptions be colored by past thoughts. Past thoughts, however persistent they may be, are only a figment of your mind.

"Stick to what is certain in every thought"
-Marcus Aurelius, Meditations, Book 8-52.

It's estimated that we have between 13,000 and 65,000 thoughts per day (feel free to look it up). Modern science has proven that even one hour after the fact, your memory of events is already not entirely reliable. It is no use defending something that is uncertain because it has lingered in your head for so long.

"All thought is a figment in your mind."

The truth is you determine which thoughts you want to have (sometimes subconsciously) and which ones bring you comfort or discomfort. These preferences differ for each person, and help you create your image of the world.

Instead of being taught to cultivate and focus on thoughts that truly matter to us, today's society bombards us with an overload of distractions, urging us to concentrate on thousands of fleeting things. Through repetition, we can change that. For example, repeating the words "Thank you" enough so that they resound naturally in your head day in and day out will make you a more grateful person in general. The practice might seem unnatural to start with but when it becomes natural, you will see your life change for the better.

The brain, so we have been told, is a muscle, and "that muscle needs to be trained." If I told you that your biceps needed to be trained, would you do bicep curls non-stop, 24 hours a day, 365 days a year? NO! Because we know that for muscles to grow stronger, alternating rest and exercise is paramount. It is exactly the same for your brain! At this very moment, your brain is overworked; give it time to rest.

How can we find mental relaxation in a world that inundates us with urgent tasks and constantly reminds us of our perceived inadequacies? It's essential to recognize that you are the master of your thoughts and not the other way around. Take control of your thinking patterns, prioritize what truly matters to you, and allow yourself moments of mental reprieve.

It has also been shown that thoughts can have a physical impact on the body, positive or negative. In the nineties, a study on cancer patients and their thoughts was carried out. In the study, the patients were asked to write their thoughts in a journal each day. The study lasted for several months. Almost all the patients who wrote down positive, uplifting thoughts were healed, whereas almost none of the patients who had written down lesser thoughts made it. Today many more studies of the sort exist, I encourage you to look them up (Google search: the power of thought in healing sick people).

By understanding the transient nature of thoughts and reclaiming your authority over them, you can navigate life with greater clarity, focus, and inner peace.

"Embrace the power to shape your thoughts consciously, directing your mind towards thoughts that uplift and inspire you."

Remember, you are in control, and your thoughts can be a force for positive transformation.

I can consciously create new thoughts by repetition of words alone. That is my super power."

Lingering On Thoughts

Feels like mind wandering but is actually mind drowning.

When we give prolonged attention to one thought, we start to identify with it. This thought begins to shape our perception of the world around us.

Take, for example, a person who thinks that people make fun of him easily. The moment that person comes across a person smiling, he is automatically going to think they are making fun of him, although people can be laughing for any reason.

Also, if when waking up in the morning, you are already thinking of a diner that same day where one of your exes will be present, that thought will make your day very difficult, except if you shake it by reminding yourself of all the other great people who are going to be there.

Lingering on a thought prevents the natural flow of your river of thought; it hinders the emergence of new thoughts, and those who emerge will only be linked to that particular thought. This is counterproductive as it prevents the exploration of diverse ideas and perspectives.

The truth is, thoughts can be summoned out of thin air, so create as many as you wish. Just reading the word "fairy," an image of a fairy can materialize in your mind. Imagine how great the inside of your mind can become if you repeat the word fairy (or any other fantasy word of your liking) over and over. You could find yourself living in a fantastical realm within your own mind, a truly marvelous experience.

"Your superpower lies in your ability to change your mind and choose what thoughts you want to entertain."

You have the power to shift your focus and let go of lingering thoughts. By doing so, you avoid becoming addicted to lingering on thoughts. Prolonged attachment to thought breeds an addiction to lingering itself, drowning any new thoughts in the stagnant river of old ones.

Remember, each thought has a fleeting existence, and only the ones we act upon gradually shape who we become and how people perceive us from the outside. The ones we linger on do shape our inner world, which can make our mind a very difficult place to live in. As humans, we are constantly changing and evolving. Our thoughts mold that evolution. Do you truly desire to be molded by the same thoughts throughout your entire life?

"Big companies are aware that repetition is key in molding the mind, which is why advertisement exists."

Repetition should be used by you daily, not to reinforce the idea that you need a new gizmo to be complete. It should be used by you to reinforce the wonderful person that you are and the person that you want to become.

If you devote excessive time to a single thought, it will occupy 100% of your mind. But you must realize that all thoughts are temporary. Remind yourself repeatedly: "This is nothing but a thought." Regardless of how negatively a thought may affect you, it is nothing but a temporary thing. You can choose to put any thought in your mind that you wish by simply repeating the words that you choose.

Challenge yourself to zoom out and gain perspective. Embrace the transient nature of thought (they never last!) and resist the allure of lingering. Free yourself from the chains of automatic thinking and create for yourself a world beyond the limits of a single thought.

Zoom In And Zoom Out

At times, our emotions can overpower us, causing us to become fixated on a thought, sometimes spiralling out of control. This is what I call zooming in, narrowing our perspective and focus, making it difficult to see the bigger picture. However, our minds are constantly generating thousands of thoughts each day, and obsessing over just one thought is unnatural and limiting.

When we zoom in, we lose sight of the vastness of our thoughts and the multitude of possibilities within any given situation. Concentrating on a single thought prevents us from exploring alternative perspectives and potential outcomes.

To fully grasp the beauty of our minds, we must learn to zoom out and maintain a broad, birds-eye view of all our thoughts.

For any given situation, there are thousands upon thousands of outcomes; concentrating or obsessing on one thought is preventing you from seeing them.

Your concentration is where you will go in your head. Your thoughts, however, are continuous, constant, and ever-flowing. By zooming in on one thought, you are wasting your time. Zoom out and learn to have a constant bird's eye view over all your thoughts.

To facilitate this zooming-out process, I invite you to practice one of the following visualization exercises. Read them first and choose the one that suits you.

The Mountain Range

Close your eyes and imagine flying over a mountain range. In the middle of this mountain range flows a river, your river of thought. This river is formed by the convergence of thousands of streams and brooks that all find their sources deep within the mountain range.

The mountain range is your mind. Each and every one of the thousands of brooks and streams flowing into your river are each and every one of the thousands of thoughts you have each day. The river is ever flowing through your mind.

Once you have this picture in your mind, you can see the troublesome thought from a much wider perspective. See how small that one stream of thought is compared to your entire mountain range and the immense flowing river in the middle of it.

This perspective reminds you of the insignificance of any single thought within the grand scheme of your mind.

Once you become good at this technique, you can even practice it with your eyes open in any circumstance life gives you. It allows you to maintain a broader perspective, regardless of the intensity of your emotions or the challenges you may be facing.

The Garden

Close your eyes and imagine a garden, a spacious open space.

In this garden, each and every plant is a thought; some are grass, and others are trees. You are a gardener walking among these plants; some of them are huge, others small, some of them are ugly, and others beautiful. You decide which ones are which and what to do with them.

As the gardener of your mind, you have a constant overview of the garden, and you know which thoughts make your garden beautiful.

Most thoughts will grow like weeds and will constantly come back, and it is up to you to notice their return and rip them out again and again (see chapter "repetition" as well).

As the gardener, you are assertive, and you know which thoughts need to be uprooted and which thoughts have the right to stay. As the gardener, you have all the tools to do so. Just as a dedicated gardener takes the time required to uproot an unwanted plant, you can eliminate any thoughts that hinder your well-being and nurture those that enhance it.

By practicing the art of zooming out, you gain a broader perspective on your thoughts and emotions. You begin to realize that a single thought does not define your entire mental landscape. Embrace the vastness of your mind and nurture it in its entirety. With an expanded viewpoint, you empower yourself to navigate through life's challenges with clarity and wisdom.

What a beautiful place this is, I like my garden.

Managing Emotions

Emotions are complex personal experiences that can be hard to describe. This chapter aims to provide two practical tools to help you navigate your emotions.

All thoughts are intertwined with emotions varying in intensity. The emotional value of a thought is the intensity of the emotion felt when you are having a particular thought.

When you allow your emotions to take control (high emotional value), your thoughts become chaotic and unfocused. On the other hand, by consciously separating emotions from your thoughts, you will slowly be able to regain control over your mind. Start by identifying the general feeling you are having, whether it is positive or negative; then, there are only a few main emotions to choose from.

There are two exercises that you can work on to deal with emotions.

The Opposite Technique (Approach)

A powerful technique to manage emotions is to identify the emotions you are experiencing and imagine the exact opposite. This technique works for all your thoughts as well.

In the book, "The Law of One," they talk about this simple way of coming to stability within yourself. In many yogic teachings, this technique is also mentioned to stabilize bad thoughts. Every time you have a thought that seems less than adequate for you, you can muster the exact opposite thought, and it will have the effect of cancelling out the negative thought.

Example 1: When you feel anger building up inside of you before talking, say to yourself I do not feel angry; I feel grateful.

Example 2: "I hate that guy for taking my job." Becomes, "I love that guy for taking my job."

Example 3: "I am ashamed of being gay" becomes "I am proud of being gay."

This practice gradually diminishes the intensity of the emotion/thought and reduces the effect of triggers over time. To make the practice easier, use the technique on everyone around you, even strangers. When you see someone who is angry on the street, say to yourself that guy is happy, for example.

Here is a list of emotions and their opposites to help you with the exercise:

- Hope: Fear
- Gratitude: Anger
- Joy: Sadness
- Pride: Shame
- Surprise: Alarm
- Love: Hate
- Desire: Disgust

Examples:

- "I hate you" becomes "I love you."
- "I am angry" becomes "I am grateful."
- "I am shameful" becomes "I am proud."
- "I am immoral" becomes "I am moral."
- "He/she is narrow-minded" becomes "He/she is open-minded."
- "He/she is timid" becomes "He/she is bold."

Of course, this is all in your head, for you to find peace of mind.

Repetition again here is essential, when you feel the anger mounting, repeat "I am grateful" over and over until the anger subsides.

The 6 Questions Technique

Even though the previous exercise can be fun to do and even funny. Some emotions and their associated thoughts may feel deeply ingrained and persistent.

In such cases, the six questions technique can be helpful. When a recurring thought emerges, ask yourself these six questions:

- Who is having this thought?
- What will happen if I let this emotion and thought continue on its course?
- When is my first memory of the thought?
- Where was the first memory of the thought?
- Why does this thought come back?
- How did this thought get in my head?

Take time to write the answers down and revisit them whenever the thought resurfaces. Through repetition, this exercise weakens the hold of these thoughts on your emotions.

Emotions are deeply personal, and each individual's journey is unique. Understanding your emotions and learning to manage them is an ongoing process. Start with the techniques discussed in this chapter; however, further exploration is highly encouraged.

Honest And Sincere Confession

Deep listening and deep expression of your feelings is the only way to get over any trauma you might have and foster true relationships with people surrounding you.

Carl Gustav Jung also states in his book "Modern Man in Search of a Soul": As soon as a man was capable of conceiving the idea of sin, repression arose. Anything that is concealed is a secret. The maintenance of secrets acts like a psychic poison that alienates their possessor from the community. (p.31)

Honest and sincere confession does not necessarily require a psychologist or psychiatrist; it can be done with a friend, a lover, a stranger, someone you trust, or anyone willing to engage in open dialogue (it will sometimes even be easier with a total stranger at a bus stop). We all have thoughts that bring us pain and thoughts that bring us joy. Unfortunately, in today's world, the weight of negative thoughts often greatly outweighs the positive ones. Do not think you are a hero by holding onto thoughts that make you feel guilt, shame, fear, anger or lust. Your self-inflicted pain is benefiting no one, especially not yourself, whatever you might be telling yourself. Sharing your deepest and darkest fears is far more courageous than holding up a mask, however heavy that mask is. It is essential to recognize that everyone, without exception, wears masks, and those who claim otherwise often wear the most elaborate ones.

"Your worst thought, the spiraling one that causes you immense pain and suffering, might be a trivial matter to someone else, and vice versa."

By announcing your intention to reveal your deepest, darkest secret and encouraging your counterpart to do the same, you create an opportunity for both of you to benefit from this exercise. Regardless of the first impression you give and the reaction you receive (it might be terrifying, shameful, horrible even), the effect of sincere confession on you will be the same: LIBERATION.

It's important to remember that what feels like an unbearable burden to you might be a non-issue for someone else (most times, that person will show you how untrue your thought was simply by their reaction). The first time is the hardest, but the more you talk about your burden, the lighter it will become.

Make it a habit to engage in this practice regularly and encourage those around you to do the same. Imagine a world where people can introduce themselves as John, someone struggling with an obsession of being inferior to others, or Julie, someone grappling with her sexual identity, instead of "John 80K per annum, sales manager" and "Julie socialite and entrepreneur." In such a world, healing and understanding would thrive.

> *"Once you have confessed what you think is the worst part of yourself, you will quickly become unshakable."*

By repeatedly, with honesty and sincerity, confessing what you think are your most terrible thoughts, you share the burden each time. Remember, your darkest thoughts are only a part of you, never your entirety. Any guilt or shame associated with these thoughts often stems from past trauma that has been inherited across generations.

If a particular thought becomes too heavy to bear, let it out. Your vulnerability and honesty will often be met with kindness and appreciation. Expressing that thought will significantly lighten the burden you carry, regardless of the outcome. While it may be scarier than severing your own hand, the liberation you experience in the aftermath of an honest and sincere confession is divine. LET IT OUT! And if need be, let out all the associated emotions in whichever way you deem fit: crying, yelling, lying down, and laughing… as long as it takes for your emotions to come back to a level you can withstand.

Eventually, you will reach a point where you can share what you once thought was the worst part of yourself with anyone, and it will have an inspiring and healing effect on you both. As more people realize the transformative power of sharing their deepest, darkest thoughts, we will finally begin to live in a society where genuine love and acceptance can flourish.

By embracing vulnerability and fearlessly expressing our innermost thoughts, we pave the way for personal growth, emotional healing, and the creation of a more compassionate world.

After confessing my deepest darkest secret, all the shame and guilt just evaporated leaving me free and light, I am not hurt by it anymore.

There Is No Bad Thought

No thought should be forbidden; instead, we should learn to process thoughts as they arise. Shame and guilt only play a role in making the thought into a monster that it absolutely is not.

Do you really think your parents, friends, idols, people that you revere... have never had one dark thought? How do you even define a dark thought when everyone's point of reference is different?

However, it is essential to consider the impact your thoughts may have before expressing them. If your thoughts have the potential to harm others, simply remain silent.

"Nothing can be clear without a polar opposite present."
-Rumi, The Essential Rumi p.220

Be thankful for all of your thoughts; how would you know which ones are good without the ones that are bad? Goodness, badness, positivity, and negativity are subjective references that vary from person to person. What one person may consider good, another may view as horrible. For example, hunters, butchers, or executioners might view killing as justified and necessary, while a vegetarian or a

Hindu may find it abhorrent. Another example is clowns; some people are terrified by them, whereas others love them.

"The dark thought, the shame, the malice, meet them at the door laughing, and invite them in. Be grateful for whoever comes, because each has been sent as a guide from beyond."
-Rumi, The Essential Rumi p. 109.

Good and bad thoughts are not separate entities; they are interconnected aspects of our minds. How could you know the good if you have never experienced the bad? From a young age, we are taught to label certain thoughts as bad and encouraged to suppress them. However, attempting to suppress thoughts only strengthens their grip on our minds. Feeding emotions of shame and guilt into a thought intensifies its presence.

All thoughts, in their essence, neutralize themselves if we let them. The ones we act upon are what make us a good or bad person, not the thoughts themselves. Consider times you may have entertained thoughts of harming someone, such as your boss. The mere presence of such thoughts does not make you a bad person; it is your conscious decision to act upon them that matters.

The only truly detrimental thing is when we allow thoughts to consume us by giving them excessive emotion and attention.

It is crucial to recognize thoughts for what they are: fleeting. By accepting all thoughts that come to us fully and acknowledging their presence without judgment, we can allow them to naturally dissipate. Spend the time needed with the thought, fully accepting it and the accompanying emotions while remaining grateful for the opportunity to experience it. If a thought lingers, it is because we have spent our lives trying to repress it. Let thoughts flow freely, and eventually, you will realize the truth that they are nothing but a thought. It is only our education and unrealistic expectations that create a monster out of something that should have only a fleeting existence: your thoughts.

> *"No tree, it is said, can grow to heaven unless its roots reach down to hell."*
> *-Carl Gustav Jung*

By adopting this perspective, we can cultivate a sense of freedom in our relationship with our thoughts. We become aware of their transient nature and no longer feel the need to suppress or judge them. Embrace the power to observe your thoughts without attaching undue significance to them, and you will discover a greater sense of peace and acceptance within yourself.

Love all of your thoughts, be thankful for them all, and little by little, more thoughts to love and be thankful for will arise.

> I am the only one that knows what thoughts I am having and how they make me feel.

> Anyone that tells me otherwise is wrong.

Breaking Free From The Chains Of Compulsive Worrying

Worrying is a habitual pattern of constantly anticipating negative outcomes and catastrophizing situations. By engaging in worry, we fixate solely on problems and pile them upon each other when they may not exist in reality.

> *"Worrying is a form of suffering that amplifies our fears and anxieties."*

It stems from unresolved past traumas that generate a sense of unease within us. In an attempt to alleviate this internal pain, our minds project these fears onto future events and other people, often envisioning the worst possible outcomes. However, this only perpetuates our anxious thoughts and further feeds our worrisome mindset.

It is important to recognize that worrying not only causes personal suffering but also has the potential to create the reality we fear. Our thoughts have the power to shape our experiences and influence the outcomes we encounter. By constantly envisioning negative scenarios, we inadvertently contribute to the manifestation of those very outcomes.

"Worrying is like paying a debt you don't owe." - Mark Twain

Worrying is a burden that only compounds our suffering. Rather than succumbing to worry, it is essential to take proactive action. Instead of just worrying, do something, acknowledge your worries as projections of unresolved trauma, and find ways to address and heal those underlying issues.

An exercise that can be productive to tackle worrying is writing down the things you worry about. Make a habit of dating and writing the worries that you have and the moments you have them. Once they are written down, they are somewhat out of your brain, and you can decide if there is something you can do about them now. If there is nothing you can do about them now, let them rest on the piece of paper and no longer in your head since there is nothing you can do about them anyway. Once your worries are written down, you can come back to them days or weeks later and see if they were really worth it or not.

There is one great source of worry that you can certainly not do anything about what other people think about you. Whatever you might think they are thinking about you, you are always going to be wrong. Most of the time, other people are too busy with their own lives to even give you one thought. So just stop thinking that you know what others think about you; every time you find yourself doing this, STOP YOURSELF IN YOUR TRACKS.

> *"Always remember, if there is nothing you can do about it now, don't worry; if there is something you can do about it now, do it."*

Breathing Consciously

In this chapter, we will explore the importance of conscious breathing and its profound impact on our body's emotions and overall well-being. Despite the vital role that oxygen plays in our lives, we are rarely taught how to breathe properly. By gaining control over our breath, we can gain control over our body, emotions, thoughts, and, ultimately, the outcomes of various situations.

You are never obliged to answer directly to provocation or anything for that matter; you can always take one breath or two. Those two breaths will give you the time to calm your racing mind.

Your breath will always be a symptom of the way you are feeling: shallow and fast when you are stressed, deep and slow when you are calm. By consciously changing your breath you can change your mood as well.

Conscious breathing is the best way to get back to a state of calm. Most people spend their entire lives not paying one bit of attention to their breathing. Not realizing the power that breathing has over the body and especially the mind.

The 1, 2 Technique

Simply pay attention to your breath and keep a mental count of one and two for the in and out breath.

- Breathe in, saying 1 mentally, during the entire in-breath (ooooooonnnnnnnneeeeee).
- Breathe out, saying 2 mentally, during the entire out-breath (twwwwoooooooo).
- Repeat as long as needed.

The 1 to 10 Technique

It is a great method for deepening breath awareness and promoting relaxation.

For this technique, it is better to be alone to practice it at first.

Here, you are counting only the in-breath up to ten mentally; once you have reached ten, you count the out-breath up to ten mentally.

One cycle will be like this:

- Breathe in, saying 1 mentally, breathe out
- Breathe in, saying 2 mentally, breathe out
- Breathe in, saying 3 mentally, breathe out
- Breathe in, saying 4 mentally, breathe out

- Breathe in, saying 5 mentally, breathe out
- Breathe in, saying 6 mentally, breathe out
- Breathe in, saying 7 mentally, breathe out
- Breathe in, saying 8 mentally, breathe out
- Breathe in, saying 9 mentally, breathe out
- Breathe in, saying 10 mentally, breathe out
- One breath in without count
- Breathe out, saying 1 mentally, breathe in
- Breathe out, saying 2 mentally, breathe in
- Breathe out, saying 3 mentally, breathe in
- Breathe out, saying 4 mentally, breathe in
- Breathe out, saying 5 mentally, breathe in
- Breathe out, saying 6 mentally, breathe in
- Breathe out, saying 7 mentally, breathe in
- Breathe out, saying 8 mentally, breathe in
- Breathe out, saying 9 mentally, breathe in
- Breathe out, saying 10 mentally, breathe in
- One breath out without count

Whenever you get lost, just start again from 1. There is no goal to attain, nor is there pressure to make many cycles. Just keep on doing it until you have reached your desired state of calm.

The Narration Technique

Sit comfortably, close your eyes, and mentally repeat the sequence:

1. "Now I am inhaling" for the in-breath
2. "Now I am exhaling" for the out-breath

Train yourself to do this exercise mentally when you are calm. Then, you will be able to use it at will when things get out of control inside and outside your head.

When you are out of control, your breath will be fast and shallow with almost no suspension between in-breath and out-breath; start the exercise immediately once you feel your thoughts getting out of control, and slowly bring the suspensions to 1 second without it feeling like suffocating.

Then you realize that you are much calmer.

The Detailed Breathing Technique

In your mind, try to concentrate not only on your natural breath but also on as many aspects of it as you can:

- The in-breath:
    - Does it feel hot, or cold;
    - Is it shallow or deep;
    - Does it feel like my belly is moving;
    - or my shoulders;

-
    - or the middle of my chest;
    - Where does the impulse for my breath come from?;
    - Am I thinking "breathe," or am I just letting it happen;
    - Am I breathing in through the nose or the mouth;
    - Does it feel like one nostril is taking more in than the other…
- The pause:
    - Is it long?
    - Or short?
    - Is there a pause?
    - Is it longer on the out-breath or the in-breath…
- The out-breath:
    - Does it feel hotter or colder than the in-breath,
    - Is it shallow or deep,
    - Where does the movement come from?
        - the stomach,
        - Or the ribs
        - Or the shoulders,

- Is it coming out of my mouth or my nose
  - Is one nostril being used more than another…

So Ham

So Ham is a Hindu mantra meaning "I am it, I am bliss eternal" in Sanskrit. In Vedic philosophy, it means identifying with the universe.

This powerful mantric breathing reminds us constantly that we are part of something bigger, and we have control over our reactions to the things that happen in our lives.

- Every time you breathe in, say mentally "So" for as long as the in-breath lasts.
- Every time you breathe out, say mentally "Ham" for as long as the breath lasts.

Conclusion - Breathing

All of the above techniques can be repeated at any time of day or night. In the subway, in front of your boss when surrounded by people, at home, with friends... Whenever you feel your mind start to race out of control, bring it back with these simple breathing techniques. The more you use them, the more efficient they become.

The only goal is to bring your racing mind to a calm state. By practicing these exercises, you will certainly gain mental clarity and serenity. Again, you can practice them any time.

We should all integrate conscious breathing into our daily lives, using it as a buffer in moments of stress, overwhelm, or anxiety. It has a profound impact on our well-being. By becoming conscious of our breath, we can gain control over our body and mind. It serves as an anchor in challenging moments and day-to-day. It is a powerful tool that is always available to us, enabling us to navigate life's ups and downs with greater ease.

After all, breathing is the most important aspect of our survival.

Becoming Conscious Of Thought

By becoming conscious of our thoughts, we can elevate our level of awareness and take control of our mental landscape. Through the practice of introspection and regular reflection, we can learn to discern our thoughts, identify their origins, and shape them according to our desires.

This will not be easy at first, but with practice, you will become the observer of your thoughts more and more rather than drowning in them.

In his beautiful book "Chatter: The Voice in Our Head, Why It Matters, and How to Harness It," Ethan Kross mentions a great way to start becoming conscious of our thoughts, especially the heavier ones.

Talk to yourself using your full name rather than using "I."
-Kross, 2021

He further explains that "I" puts you right in the middle of the thought, whereas using your name will give you a fly-on-the-wall perspective of your thought.

Try it right now; "I am going to the supermarket," becomes "Lee Smith is going to the supermarket." Then, with more profound thoughts, "I am miserable because I just got dumped," becomes "Lee Smith is miserable because he/she just got dumped." It gives a sense of perspective, enabling you to see the thought from a distance.

By dedicating moments of stillness and reflection each day, we can shine a light on the thoughts that arise within us. Through this process, we begin to distinguish between thoughts that align with our intentions and those that do not. We observe the thoughts we consciously cultivate, as well as thoughts that seem to enter our minds spontaneously.

It is especially important to identify the ones that make you feel bad. When you feel these thoughts spiraling out of control, take a moment and write them down same as the worrisome thoughts.

This practice may be initially challenging, but it is far from impossible. With repetition and patience, we can sharpen our ability to categorize thoughts into groups. By recognizing our thoughts and being able to notice the moment they arise, we become participants in shaping our inner world and, thus, our outer world.

Free yourself from self-judgment, embrace all aspects of yourself, and acknowledge your role as the creator of your own experience. Bring your thoughts into your conscious awareness, shine a light on the beautiful ones as well as the ones that make you feel less beautiful, and open the door to self-transformation.

Take self-judgment out of the picture; Imagine it is your best friend or a loved one who is telling you the thought. Would your reaction be different?

The Power of Vocabulary

Your mind is the same as your body; feed your body with junk, and you will feel like junk. Feed your mind with junk words, and your mind will create junk thoughts.

"All that we are is the result of what we have thought. We are made of our thoughts; we are molded by our thoughts."
- The Buddha

The vocabulary we use has immense power over our minds and, therefore, our reality. Using positive and uplifting words can have a transformative effect on our thoughts and experiences.

Consider the simple word "spoon". When you think of the word spoon, it automatically activates a network of associated thoughts: soup, hot, bowl, cutlery, table, eating, food, cereals, yogurt, mornings, and so on. Similarly, when you think of the word "mountain," it triggers thoughts related to snow, hikes, storms, immense vastness… The vocabulary we use has the power to evoke memories, emotions, and mental imagery.

While some words may slip out involuntarily, for most people, the words we choose to speak are within our conscious control. By making a deliberate effort to use fewer "bad" words (such as negative, derogatory, harsh language, and swear words), we can positively influence our thoughts and shape our reality.

Instead of Fuck, use Flipper; instead of Shit, use Schnitzel people will get the message all the same!

You can notice who a person truly is by the vocabulary that they use; next time someone is having a casual conversation with you, pay attention to the vocabulary they are choosing to use to describe people and circumstances rather than paying attention to who or what they are describing. Words are the reflection of how individuals are feeling and perceiving the world around them.

Choosing certain words over others will have a profound impact not only on your thoughts but the circumstances of your life. By consciously choosing positive, empowering, and uplifting words, you can create a more optimistic and constructive mindset, which in turn will attract more positive experiences and opportunities into your life.

Words have the power to shape our perceptions, influence our thoughts, and ultimately impact our reality. Embrace the understanding that the vocabulary you use is a tool for creating a more positive and fulfilling life. Choose your words mindfully, and watch as your thoughts and circumstances align with the energy and intention behind them.

Hereafter is a list of some "good words" for you to use at will (use at least one a day):

Abundance	Fresh	Proud
Adorable	Friendly	Quality
Awesome	Fun	Quiet
Beautiful	Genuine	Ready
Bliss	Good	Reliable
Brave	Great	Reward
Brilliant	Honest	Safe
Calm	Impressive	Secure
Celebrate	Innovative	Soulful
Charming	Joy	Super
Cool	Kind	Thriving
Delight	Laughing	Trusting
Divine	Legendary	Truthful
Earnest	Lucky	Upbeat
Electrifying	Marvellous	Upright

Energetic	Miraculous	Vigorous
Excellent	Okay	Vibrant
Exquisite	Optimistic	Welcome
Exciting	Pleasant	Willing
Fabulous	Positive	Wondrous
Fine	Progress	Yes

Repetition rather than repression

"Your mind will take on the character of your most frequent thoughts: Souls are dyed by thoughts. So dye your own with a succession of thoughts like these. For example: where life can be lived, so can a good life."
- Marcus Aurelius, Meditations, Book 5-16.

Repetition of a thought rather than repression of another can be a powerful tool in shaping your reality. You are not defined by any single thought, but your thoughts do have the ability to influence your actions, words, and circumstances. By actively choosing which thoughts to focus on, you can exercise control over your mind. This choice is made by repeating a word or a phrase until it becomes part of you.

This is a practically identical practice to repeating a mantra. Mantras are words or phrases that you repeat to yourself on a regular basis in order to shift your mindset. Some descriptions go as far as to say it had a transformative effect on the mind of the individual reciting it. Any word or phrase repeated can be a mantra. They do not necessarily have to be Sanskrit or sacred utterances. They only have to be sacred for you. They only have to have a personal and positive meaning that resonates with you.

"Accept that things will never be exactly the way you thought they would be."

Repetition of words is a technique that can help bring a specific thought to the forefront of your mind. By simply repeating a word or a phrase, you can make a particular thought arise spontaneously. This practice gives your mind a momentary break and allows clarity to emerge.

Create a short list of words or phrases that you love or that evoke feelings of joy, peace, or any positive emotion. Read this list repeatedly (especially when getting up in the morning) until your mind becomes filled with those uplifting words. Keep the list with you at all times until you have it committed to memory. This practice can be used at will and especially whenever difficult thoughts emerge. Even if you are only able to repeat one word from the list over and over, you are making progress.

Using The Three Simple Words, I...LOVE...YOU

1. Repressing thoughts can often backfire, as they gain more power over you the harder you try to forget them. Instead, embrace repetition as a means to redirect your focus and replace unwanted thoughts altogether. Closing

your eyes and repeating the words "I love you" (or any other positive/uplifting words) for 30 seconds, then wait. Do you feel the profound effect that the three words can have on your state of mind?

2. This next exercise using "I love you" is fun and can even be funny. During your day, whenever you see someone, anyone, look at them and in your mind say, "I love you." Do this with everyone you see, in the subway, at work, at home…

3. Another exercise you can practice to notice the power of repetition is the following: When you are about to meet someone you despise or loathe, but you have to meet him or her for work or another obligation, make a mental image in your head of that person and say to it: "I LOVE YOU" over and over as many times as you can.

Through the power of repetition, you can gradually reshape your thoughts and create a mental environment that aligns with your desires and values. Embrace this practice, and let the limitless power of words guide you towards a more positive and fulfilling life. In the beginning, doing these activities will be hard; your mind will wander, and you will quickly forget the repetition. When you remember, start

the activity again. Do not get angry at yourself. You are making progress.

Forgive

Forgiveness is a profound act of liberation and healing that can transform your life. It involves getting rid of resentment, anger, and the desire for revenge towards those who have caused you harm. They might have caused you harm for a myriad of reasons; sometimes, they don't even know they hurt you.

"Holding onto hate is like drinking poison and hoping the other person will die." - Unknown.

By forgiving, you free yourself from the burdens of negative emotions and create space for healing and personal growth.

Forgive your parents, enemies, and those who harmed you; holding onto grudges only weighs you down and prolongs your suffering. Remember, forgiveness is not about condoning their actions but about releasing yourself from the pain they caused.

Vindictiveness only perpetuates negativity and prevents you from finding peace and happiness.

You can also seek forgiveness for your own shortcomings; there are moments in your life where you could have been a better person, acknowledge your mistakes, and take responsibility for them. Asking for forgiveness can be challenging as it requires opening up and showing your vulnerabilities. Be prepared for the possibility that the response will probably not meet your expectations. Nevertheless, seeking forgiveness is important for your own healing.

If you find the strength within you to do this, ask for forgiveness from people who have hurt you. The pain that people inflict on others is but a glimpse of the suffering and pain that they themselves go through every day. You somehow are also part of that suffering in their hearts. Forgiveness can open the road for the healing of both parties.

Asking for forgiveness and forgiveness will release the hold that hatred and fear have on you. Hatred and fear towards someone only imprisons you in your own mind. Remember, forgiving does not mean forgetting or necessarily reconciling with the person, but it will release you from negative emotions.

In order to make the process of forgiveness easier, a great morning ritual is the following (the people concerned do not even have to be present):

Ask for forgiveness and forgive as well, e.g. "Father, I ask for your forgiveness for not being the son/daughter you wanted me to be, AND I forgive you for not being the father I wanted you to be." Repeat this ritual over and over, starting with all the members of your family and your relation to them and spreading out to all of your acquaintances.

This ritual helps cultivate forgiveness and sets a positive tone for the day.

Forgiveness is a personal journey; it may take time and effort to fully embrace it. Be patient and compassionate with yourself. Remember, by choosing forgiveness, you free yourself from the chains of resentment and open the door to inner peace and happiness.

The Ho'oponnoppono "Prayer"

The Ho'oponnopono prayer, originating from the Hawaiian culture, embodies the essence of forgiveness, healing, and love. Its simple yet profound words, "Sorry," "Please forgive me," "Thank you," and "I love you," hold the power to shift our thoughts and emotions.

The power of words is undeniable, and "Sorry," "Thank you," and "I love you" carry immense significance in fostering healing, gratitude, and love in our lives. By embracing these words and incorporating them into our daily practice, we can cultivate a profound transformation within ourselves and our relationships.

When faced with negative or troubling thoughts, repeating the Ho'oponnoppono prayer can serve as a powerful tool to redirect focus and release the grip of those thoughts. It goes beyond assigning blame or seeking reason; instead, it invites us to take responsibility for our thoughts, emotions, and experiences. Through sincere repetition, we allow ourselves to let go, and cultivate a loving mindset.

Remember, healing is a process. By constantly repeating the words, you can gradually dissolve the weight of challenging thoughts and replace them with feelings of forgiveness, gratitude, and love.

Whenever you find yourself caught in the grip of negative thoughts, remember the power of these words and use them as a tool to shift your mindset and embrace a more positive and compassionate perspective.

Be Thankful

For everything that happens to you, good and bad, Be thankful. Do this for one person and one person only: yourself.

Being grateful for everything that happens to us, both the good and the bad, can have a profound impact on our well-being and outlook in life. Be thankful for all the things that you can do or that you will do for all the things in your life that surround you.

Gratitude has the power to reshape your mindset entirely; it will help you find meaning and appreciation in every experience.

"The defining characteristic of a good person is to love and embrace whatever happens to him."
- Marcus Aurelius (Meditations 3-16-2).

Embracing gratitude will help you to see hidden lessons and growth potential in challenging times and overcome negativity. Expressing gratitude has a positive influence on your relationships and interactions, as well as spreading positivity to others around you. The key here is to start small and to say thank you for things that we take for granted.

- Are you alive? Say, thank you.
- Can you read? Say, thank you.
- Can you taste? Say, thank you.
- Can you hear? Say, thank you.
- Can you feel? Say, thank you.
- Can you think? Say, thank you.
- Can you see? Say, thank you.
- Can you touch? Say, thank you.
- Can you love? Say, thank you.
- Can you walk? Say, thank you.
- Can you sleep? Say, than you.

Making a habit out of this will greatly improve your general outlook on life.

By practicing saying "thank you" every day and embracing gratitude in our daily lives, we can shift our perspective, find appreciation in every moment, and unlock a deeper sense of happiness and contentment. When the word "thank you" is constantly resounding in your head, your mind ceases to race left and right, allowing it time to relax as well.

Gratitude has the potential to positively impact ourselves and those around us. Say "thank you" with honesty and sincerity, and watch its effects ripple throughout your life.

"Let not your mind run on what you lack as much as on what you have already." - Unknown.

Stop Complaining And Let Go Of The Need To Be Right

Complaining serves no purpose other than to drain your energy and focus on the problems rather than the solutions. It's time to break free from the habit of complaining and start using your mind as a tool to create a new reality where every problem is seen as a potential solution.

"Our life is shaped by our mind; we become what we think." – Buddha.

When you complain, you fixate on the source of the problem, keeping your focus on negativity. Instead, shift your mindset towards finding solutions and opportunities. Train your mind to see challenges as stepping stones for growth and development.

Complaining not only wastes your energy and mental capacity but also consumes your time. It hinders your ability to enjoy the present moment and blinds you to the possibilities surrounding you.

Make a conscious decision to stop complaining right now and free yourself from this unproductive habit.

Here's a simple exercise: Whenever something happens that might trigger a complaint, choose gratitude instead. Be thankful for the lessons you can learn from the situation or the potential dangers you managed to avoid. For instance, if you experience a minor accident, consider how it potentially prevented a potentially more significant accident in the future. This shift in perspective might seem trivial, but it's a powerful truth:

"The Universe will never burden you with something you cannot handle."

Additionally, closely related to complaining is the need to be right. They both have roots in unresolved trauma. Let go of the urge to always be right in every argument or situation. The need to prove your point can be exhausting and lead to unnecessary conflicts.

Embrace humility and openness to different perspectives. Remember, it is more important to maintain healthy relationships and seek understanding than to assert your ego.

Self-improvement can be done by working from the inside out as well as from the outside in. RETAIN YOUR

NEED TO COMPLAIN AND TO BE RIGHT, and they will fade away eventually.

By releasing the habit of complaining and relinquishing the need to be right, you create space for peace, gratitude, and growth in your life. Embrace this transformative shift and watch as your mindset and interactions with others become more positive and fulfilling.

The Five Senses and Thought

Our five senses play a crucial role in how we perceive and interpret the world around us. Each person's interpretation is heavily influenced by their past experiences. What might evoke a cherished childhood memory for one person could trigger a traumatic experience for another. Unfortunately, our senses have also been conditioned by external influences such as advertising and media, fostering a dependency on material things.

However, it is important to recognize that our thoughts are at the core of how we interpret the world through our senses. This relationship works both ways. Just as our thoughts can shape our sensory experience, we can consciously use our senses to transform our thoughts. This process occurs naturally on a daily basis, but by making it a deliberate practice, we can harness its power for positive change.

To elevate your positive thoughts, create simple rituals that engage one or more of your five senses. This practice is most effective when you fully immerse yourself in the moment and give it the time and attention it deserves. Over the course of days and weeks, you'll begin to witness the results.

Here are some sensory-focused techniques you can incorporate into your morning routine and throughout the day whenever you can:

Smell:

Have cinnamon, sandalwood, rose, or lavender essence next to your bed or any scent that brings you joy. Give it a good sniff every morning with your eyes still closed, and let yourself be transported to the memory of that beautiful scent and all the beautiful images it brings to your mind.

Sight:

Keep print pictures of your fondest memories on your bedside table. Spend one minute each morning looking at the pictures, allowing them to fill you with gratitude and positivity.

Write yourself encouraging messages the night before that you read the next day. You can also write one for each day at the beginning of the week and read it out loud. Write these when you are feeling good about yourself. Or have someone who likes you write them, and do the same for them. You can have as many as you want; it does not have to be one per day; it can be many.

Hearing:

Put on your favorite tune on full volume to start off the day and let it move you. Embrace the power of sound to uplift your mood and set the tone for the day. Does the sound of coins remind you of all the cash that you are going to make? Have a bowl with coins nearby and let them tingle!

Touch:

Explore the tactile sensations you enjoy. Do you like the feel of dollar bills? Put a couple at arm's length. Everyone loves touching something: cloth, silk, skin, a piece of wood... take the time to truly experience the sensation and connect to the material.

Taste:

Whenever possible, treat yourself to your favorite breakfast. Or indulge in a taste that brings you joy. Start your day with a flavourful experience that delights your taste buds.

By consciously practicing these sensory rituals every morning and throughout the day, fully savoring each moment, you'll begin to notice results in just a few days. For optimal effect, mix up the techniques, incorporating different senses on different days. Embrace the power of your senses to create a positive shift in your thoughts and overall well-being.

Conclusion

In conclusion, the power of thoughts is undeniable. They have the ability to shape our mental and physical well-being, as well as influence our experiences and interactions with the world.

To illustrate this, I would like to cite two stories: one is of Gem Gilbert, and the other is a story of a great sage recounted by countless spiritual teachers.

When she was little, Gem Gilbert witnessed a tragedy: her mother brought her to the dentist for a routine visit. Gem thought she and her mother would be back home in an instant. But something went terribly wrong, and the little girl watched her mother die on the dentist's seat. This traumatic memory stayed with her, and she did nothing about it.

For years, she refused to go to the dentist, which is understandable, until one day, she suffered from such an unbearable toothache, and, convinced by her family, she agreed to have a dentist come to her home to operate. However, by the time the dentist had set up all his apparatus and was ready to operate, he found Gem Gilbert dead!

The memory of Gem's mother's death was so strong that it eventually killed her. This is the power that the mind can have over you and your life. Gem Gilbert's predicament is terrible, but her fate could have been avoided had she processed the death of her mother instead of letting the memory fester in her mind. If a negative thought can have that effect, wouldn't positive thoughts possibly have an effect as strong?

There is also the story of a great sage, an illumined man, a holy man, who lived his life selflessly, bringing joy and goodness to everyone around him. When he passed away, he found himself in a place that he believed to be heaven. People were naturally drawn to him, and he effortlessly connected with them, spreading love and compassion.

However, after three years, the administrators of heaven realized their mistake. They had mistakenly sent this holy man to hell instead of heaven. Upon realizing their error, they promptly sent an official to apologize and correct the situation.

Upon the official's arrival, he expressed deep regret for the confusion and offered to take the holy man back to heaven immediately. However, the sage responded with a gentle smile, "No, thank you. I have created my own heaven right here with the people around me."

Thoughts can either be destructive, leading to anxiety, worry, and even physical ailments, or they can be empowering, uplifting, and create a positive reality. It is important to recognize that thoughts are not inherently real, but rather creations of our own minds recalled in the moment we have them. Memories, too, are thoughts of past events that can shape our present and future.

By understanding the nature of thoughts and their influence, we can take control and become the masters of our minds and lives. This involves reducing the quantity of thoughts and giving our brains time to relax. The techniques mentioned in this book offer guidance on managing thoughts, cultivating positive thinking, and ultimately creating a happier life for ourselves and those around us.

Remember, thoughts have immense power, but "We have the ability to choose which thoughts to entertain and nurture by using the techniques in this book." By harnessing this power, we can transform our lives and create a paradise within ourselves, regardless of external circumstances. Embrace the journey of self-discovery and take control of your thoughts to unlock the full potential of your mind and live a more fulfilling life.

Continue practicing everyday and you will get there, Love Always.

Bye,Bye and Safe travels!

Bibliography

Aurelius, M. (2014). *Meditations.* Milton Keynes, Great Britain: Pinguin Random House.

Jung, C. G. (1933). *Modern Man in Search of a Soul.* (W. D. Baynes, Trad.) New York: Houghton Mifflin Harcourt.

Kross, E. (2021). *Chatter: The Voice in Our Head, Why it Matters, and How to Harness It.* New York: Crown Publishing Group.

Rumi. (2004). *The Essential Rumi.* (C. Barks, Trad.) New-York: HarperCollins Publishers.

Tolle, E. (2004). *The Power of Now.* Vancouver: Namaste Publishing.

www.ingramcontent.com/pod-product-compliance
Lightning Source LLC
Chambersburg PA
CBHW050203130526
44591CB00034B/2028